Love Lessons
from My Mom

Love Lessons from My Mom

(Important Stuff I Hope I Never Forget)

by Kelly Corbet

Celestial Arts
Berkeley Toronto

Book design by VICTOR MINGOVITS, NYC

CA
Celestial Arts, P.O. Box 7123, Berkeley, California 94707
http://www.tenspeed.com
A Heart & Star Book

Original art by Breah Parker on pages 18, 22, and 28. © BliPStudio 2000.

Quotes on pages 20 and 45 from **Illusions: The Adventures of a Reluctant Messiah** by Richard Bach, copyright © 1977 by Richard Bach and Leslie Parrish-Bach. Used by permission of Dell Publishing, a division of Random House, Inc.

Quote on page 72 from **Anatomy of the Spirit** by Caroline Myss reprinted by permission of Crown Publishing Group.

Quote on page 67 from **You Can Have It All** by Arnold Patent reprinted by permission.

Author photo by Vera Photography
http://www.veraphotography.com

Distributed in Australia by Simon and Schuster Australia, in Canada by Ten Speed Press Canada, in New Zealand by Southern Publishers Group, in South Africa by Real Books, in Southeast Asia by Berkeley Books, and in the United Kingdom and Europe by Airlift Books.

Library of Congress Cataloging-in-Publication Data
Corbet, Kelly.   Love lessons from my mom: important stuff I hope I never forget / Kelly Corbet.   p. cm.
ISBN 0-89087-999-0   Conduct of life. I. Title.
BF637.C5 C66 2001   158--dc21
Printed in Singapore
First printing, 2001
1 2 3 4 5 05 04 03 02 01

To my wonderful mother, Barby Corbet Woods, who taught me
about the most important thing of all: LOVE

and

To "Swoosh," the daughter-to-be who inspired me
to remember my mom's Love Lessons.

I thank you both.

Table of Contents

Beginning Words

I got lucky in the "Mom Department," and I wish everyone could be so fortunate (including my own kids). To that end, I wrote this book about the Love Lessons that my **amazing** mother has lived and taught.

In focusing on her Fabulous Parenting Examples, the essence of all her individual lessons finally dawned on me:

Opportunities to learn about Love are all around us, just waiting to be invited in!

**Love isn't so much dependent on a person
as it is on an attitude...an attitude of
joy and expectancy.**

That's what Mom taught me in everything she did.

Now, if this doesn't strike you as a Major Big Deal, think about it for another minute, please. What better gift to give a child than the ability to see the possibility of joy in every experience? While growing up, that person stays so busy looking for all the Good Stuff, that he or she ends up creating their own Great Life—rather than expecting someone else to do it. (After all, what you expect, you invite.)

This can be **very important information** along the path of Life because, it turns out, a Love Lesson can show up in a variety of (often surprising) outfits. And we might not know to call it a "Love Lesson" unless we are prepared.

A Love Lesson can come dressed as a baggage handler or a bag lady, a family counselor or a drive-you-nuts member of your family. A Love Lesson might even come in the shape of a flower growing in the backyard. It's all in the invitation. So if you're open, there's no telling what great joys you'll have over for tea or meet in a parking lot.

This whole concept goes a long way in explaining how, exactly, my mom passed on so many **Joy-Is-Everywhere** messages. How she made me feel so loved. How she showed me Life's adventures everywhere:

in a library visit

a garden

a rainy-day
after-school
treat

Way too many adults are still mad at their parents for sins (mostly, it seems, of omission) committed eons ago. Really, how many dinner party conversations and best-selling books center on just this topic?

"I hated it when my mom yelled at my friends. Nobody ever wanted to play at my house!"

"My mother always made me eat everything on my plate, even if that meant a morning rerun."

"My dad never came to my piano recitals."

And what about the years of psychotherapy required—perhaps by children **and** their parents—for well-intended-but-nevertheless-crummy choices? I don't want my kids to go to therapy over my stupidity...or, even worse, my

FORGETFULNESS

So I'm writing as much as I remember about my mom's continuous Love Lessons. Maybe this little book will help me be a more loving parent.

To be ready for Love Lessons, or rather, to invite them in, my mom kept two sayings handy at all times:

**Everything happens
for a Reason.**

-AND-

**We're all just here to
love each other.**

Or, as I was just saying, **"Love is always out there; it just needs an invitation."**

I invite you to read my notes. Maybe they'll help you create your own opening for Love's Lessons. If you picked up this book and have gotten this far, there may just be a Reason...

The Big R: RESPECT

When I started this project, I went right to The Source and flat-out asked: "Mom, what *do* you think made you such a great mother?"

Over the phone she responded, "I guess it would have to be respect. I always thought of you girls as 'real' people, and that I should treat you like I would any friend I respected."

That was it? One common, little, everyday word—**respect**—to explain how she helped produce three well-adjusted daughters? Initially, I was pretty disappointed with her answer. It seemed

way too simplistic

to describe what was really amazing in hindsight.

And, besides, she didn't even mention the love part, which I always had assumed was the most important ingredient.

Then I thought about it more...

Sure. Almost all parents out there love their kids. I have no doubt that my grandmother loved my mother. She didn't always treat her so nicely, though, and she did not treat her like a friend.

OK, maybe **RESPECT** wasn't something to be taken lightly here.

I started to consider how Mom's respect manifested itself in my day-to-day life. One example that came to mind was how many times she would ask my opinion...

In situations where most parents would have given their children

my mother would ask me what I supposed was the right thing to do. We'd discuss the reasons and come up with a kid-generated (rather than parent-commanded) resolution. Then—this is **BIG**—she respected my conclusion.

Sometimes, people assume that **Years on the Planet** is the magic metric for intelligence or knowledge. I haven't found a direct correlation there. In fact, sometimes the opposite seems more true: as we get older but not necessarily wiser, our "been there, done that" assumptions might block some **Real Information** from getting through. Years-here "wisdom" is a whole lot heavier for us adults than it is for a hardly-been-here-long-enough-to-form-a-bias kindergartner, for example.

And so my mom must have understood that concept—enough to let me make my own decisions (and occasional mistakes). Maybe she knew somehow that respecting a young person's innate knowledge really **IS** one of the most important keys to good parenting.

I think part of the reason Mom came to this **Respect Conclusion** is that she didn't receive much respect from her own mother while growing up. She never felt that her opinions mattered, and she didn't get to do a whole lot of choosing about her own life. She promised herself to do things differently when she was a mommy. Fortunately for me, she did.

Doing things "differently," though, isn't always as easy as it sounds. I mean, you can know what you **DON'T** like to do or be, but homing in on the huge realm of possibilities of what you **MIGHT** like to do or be can be pretty daunting. This is one of the reasons I think Mom's lessons are so astonishing. My mom literally found these answers—these ways of doing and being—inside herself! That's pretty good news, as far as I'm concerned, because it means we all have some pretty insightful (literally in-sight-full...get it?) answers about how we should be and could be at our very best. All we have to do is look within! (And maybe reading a few books like this one won't hurt, either.)

Imagination vs. Reality

I was about three years old when my parents had a humongous-al-the-time picture painted of me. As soon as I met the artist, panic struck:

"How will he know how to paint Paulette, Mom?!?!?"

(Paulette was my imaginary pet mouse and best friend who went everywhere with me. She and my mom got along great, too...I could tell by their interesting conversations. This artist, though, had me worried. He had never met Paulette before; how was he going to see her?)

Without a moment of hesitation, Mom responded, first to me,

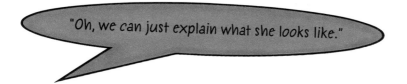

"Oh, we can just explain what she looks like."

(Immediate relief descended on me.)

To the artist, she carefully described my lap-sitting, large, white mouse-friend. The description enabled him to place the not-so-petite Paulette smack dab in the middle of his artwork.

Now, so many years later, what thrills me more than a pale mouse in the center of a painting is that my mom recognized the importance of my imaginary friend. In a moment of **creative go-for-it-ism** (made permanent by the painter's long-since-dry brush strokes), my mother demonstrated her belief in my creativity.

And all without a moment of hesitation. I don't know how many mothers would have said,

"Oh no, dear, Paulette is just imaginary."

(As if imaginations weren't the first step in creating reality!?!)

But I suspect the mothers who would point out Paulette's nonvisible aspects are probably in the majority. Not through any malice on their part, of course. It's probably because they place more importance on what things look like—or are supposed to look like—than what they might possibly, truly BE.

I have well-meaning friends who won't put their kid-decorated cookies on the holiday buffet table because the cookie craftsmanship doesn't look like the pictures in the cookbooks. It's as if they believe the kid form of expression is less valuable than what the world views as "correct," or "pretty," or "normal."

I credit my mother's full-speed-ahead belief in my own creativity as an enormous factor in helping me dare to go in directions the world doesn't necessarily call "correct," or "pretty," or "normal."

Like attending grad school when I was already "old." Or starting my own business when **The Experts** said I was crazy. And maybe, even, like writing this book. (After all, it's common knowledge that it is **VERY DIFFICULT** for an "unknown" to get a book published.)

To my mom, my visions and creations have always been real. And that made them even more real for me. Mom always believed that "perception creates reality."

In Richard Bach's book, **ILLUSIONS**, he writes,

"Argue for your limitations, and sure enough, they're yours."

The corollary, I think, is true as well:

"Open up your imagination to POTENTIAL, and sure enough, it's yours."

More recently than the Paulette incident, I learned another big lesson about the power of believing in one's own creations. In a strategy course at Harvard Business School (taught by a very wise and wonderful Professor Hax), we studied all kinds of business enterprises that, using **Pure Business Logic**, never should have succeeded (business models, profitability potential, critical success factors, blah, blah, blah). Companies like Saturn and USA Today, for example, have "made it" in spite of the odds and the competition largely due to the vision and creativity of their leaders. These insightful corporate gurus gave power to their creativity and made their ideas real.

I wonder how **they** learned to do that?

I Can Do Anything

Mom taught me to believe in myself, that I was a capable person. She didn't so much tell me as she actually believed in me. That, in itself, was pretty empowering.

Even in the fourth grade, I **"just knew"** I could do anything. I believed I could make wise decisions, and my mom would back me up (this ties into the respect thing, I see).

Like what to wear.

I remember opening my closet before school and thinking: "I can wear **ANYTHING** I want to school! Jean's mom doesn't let her choose."

Of course, I didn't know then what a true

Mom had given me. (She admits today that letting me out of the house in those shiny blue plastic-and-cork platform clogs was "challenging.")

It was only recently, as a so-called adult, when people said things like,

"How can you **DO** that?"

-OR-

"Wow, that's brave of you!"

that I have remembered in an out-loud way,

I CAN DO ANYTHING !

Thus inspired by my mom, I learned that we are all "The Big Choosers," "The Master Inventors" of our lives, and we can—each one of us—create the life we want. I guess other people's mothers must not have known that, since I see a lot of grown-ups who aren't creating joy-filled realities for themselves now.

I'm sure I forget some of those

I CAN DO ANYTHING !

thoughts sometimes, too. After all, Life doesn't generally encourage us to think in daring, blue-cork clog ways. (Oh, how grateful I am to have been blessed with a mother capable of disregarding good fashion sense for the sake of a daughter's good self-image!)

Decisions, Decisions

Before bed, Mom would always read us stories, or even better, she would make them up with us on a felt storyboard. The main storyboard character was Winky Bear, and of course, he had family members and friends take part in his performances.

Winky Bear was a moralistic kind of guy. He always seemed to be faced with an ethical dilemma that required **DEEP THOUGHT** and **DISCUSSION**.

Fortunately, my sisters and I were there to help guide him through his moral swamp. We would talk over the decisions and actions he should make in his predicament-of-the-day (and I'm certain—with our assistance—he always did THE RIGHT THING).

For example, in one scene, Winky Bear accused his brother of taking his favorite ball, only to remember later that he, himself, had left the ball at school. Winky immediately apologized and took **responsibility** for his own actions (just as we had advised him to do).

As much as we believed we were helping Winky Bear, I suspect we were the ones who really gained from these exercises. We learned to identify and articulate moral issues. And probably more important, we learned the value of thinking out solutions for ourselves, rather than going with what might be perceived as expedient or "popular."

Years later, Mom taught Decision Making in public schools. As far as I know, Winky Bear and his flat, felt friends were not course participants, but they could have been. The premise of the course was to get preteens in dialogue around **sticky situations**. The plan was that by developing their decision-making skills under no-pressure scenarios, they would be better prepared when more important, life-affecting decisions came up (such as taking drugs).

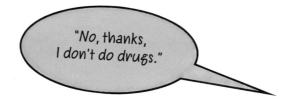

I remember reading the course evaluations from both parents and students. The class was popular, which was clear in the reviews. What surprised me, though, was how many participants wrote that they had never before thought about their decisions, or how they went about making them! I guess they'd never helped Winky Bear.

Winky Bear bedtimes weren't the only chances Mom offered to help us with decision-making skills. And I sure am glad. Having faith in my own good skills in the choices arena has given me **confidence**; it validates my voice (both inner voice and the kind everyone else can hear), and empowers me still.

What Chance Do They Have?

My dad is a very open-hearted man. He smiles, waves, and says "hi" to absolutely everyone. Going somewhere with him is like being in a parade. He's a real egalitarian, too. Growing up, I could never distinguish by his mannerisms whether he was talking on the phone to a client in jail or to the state governor. Status has never affected the way he sees or treats people. He's definitely **NOT** a snob.

I cannot always claim to display the same generous characteristic. I remember getting a serious dose of Dad's un-snobbiness that makes me blush even now.

One day at a stoplight (I was about nine years old), I looked at the muffler-free pickup smoking up a storm right next to our car. The truck was filled with dirty, raggedy-looking kids. And the parents weren't likely to show up on any Best Dressed lists, either.

I was just sure these ragtags were destined for a future of "ragtagginess." As I stared into the next lane, I wondered out loud: "What chance in life do those poor children have?"

Good thing we were already stopped, or I could have been the cause of a family whiplash attack. My father, who seldom raised his voice, clenched the steering wheel and, looking at his alien daughter, commanded:

"Never talk like that, Kelly! You can never tell how someone might end up just by how poor they are when they start out. Look at me!"

This man of humble beginnings was very serious (a rare event). And he was right (a more frequent event). And, boy, was I red-faced.

That afternoon in the car left an immense impression on my germinating character. I'm not saying I never judge by looks—I'm still working on that lesson—but often when I do start down that path, I find myself sitting in the front seat of our old station wagon, and I hear my dad's voice.

Gratefulness Galore

When we were little, my mom created a "Chores Chart" for each of her three daughters. It listed our daily duties and included a section to check off what we completed every day. The chores were tailored to our different ages, but one responsibility we all had in common was to

say our prayers reverently

What a powerful experience that was! Every evening, not only did we get to review our accomplishments (complete with gold stars), but we took time to be thankful for each other and the wonderful things we might have experienced that day.

Weekly Chores Chart

Chore	S	M	T	W	T	F	S
Make my bed							
Brush my teeth							
Feed Ginger							
Get along with sisters							
Put away my toys							
Say prayers reverently							

I realize now that a big part of our prayers involved counting our blessings.

1 2 3 4 5 6

I consider this a **VERY IMPORTANT Love Lesson**. Here's why. Often, people send their prayers in one basic direction: **"Dear God, please..."** But my mom taught me the importance of saying, **"Dear God, thank you..."** * These are very different messages, both to the Universe and to ourselves.

I'm not saying the first message is "bad," but I do think the thankful version helps us appreciate the abundance already in our lives, instead of what we lack. I also think it helps us create **more abundance.** **

I know a woman who does a lot of anti-gratefulness focusing. She moans that she is "the poorest" of all her friends, and she actually complains about gifts she receives! OK, we've all come by a present or

* I don't think it's important what we call the Ultimate Creative Power in the Universe. What's important is keeping a connection and remembering He/She/It is always there.

** Just to be clear with my definition here: abundance isn't just about material stuff. Being abundant means you have lots of joy, laughter, friends, happy times—whatever you consider valuable—in your life.

two that shocked us, but this woman gripes about practically **EVERY** gift she gets. I think she's been sending out those ungrateful poor-me messages for so many years that the Universe has had no choice but to respond in kind. (Her life does seem to have more trauma and drama than the norm.) If it's true, as I suspect, that what you focus on expands, then she's got her microscope on the wrong stuff.

On the other side of the stream, an actor I once saw on a talk show was asked whether he set aside time to pray every day. The man responded that he hoped his **whole life was a prayer**. He tried to keep the prayer part and the living part very connected, and he tried to make everything he did be about gratefulness. It's been eons since I heard that interview, but his message really stuck with me.

What would it be like to **always** be thankful for the good stuff? I hope I teach myself to find out!

Behavior As Blueprint

Looking back, Mom's unself-conscious kindness toward the world seems just as character-molding as how she treated me. Take Ollie from the halfway house, for instance. Mom met him while volunteer-teaching in a prison. Once free, or halfway free, my mother paid him to do occasional chores around the house so he could save up some money.

I don't remember feeling threatened by him (though I suspect I remained ignorant of his former line of work). He looked a little different from my parents' friends, but my mom treated him the same way she treated everyone else, so there was no need to feel concerned.

She reminded me regularly that

We are ALL
Children of the
Universe

and therefore are all special. No exceptions. That means we should treat everybody (and her term for everybody was definitely **UN**conditional) like they really are special. Furthermore, if we always

33

treat people like they're great, they remember how great they are and act like it!

Ollie was a good example of the living-up-to-goodness expectations Mom set...for me and for all those around her. That Ollie came to our home to build up his cash flow and his self-worth was also proof that she really lived and acted what she taught us.

BE KIND TO EVERYONE

I've seen more than a few parents profess one thing and behave as if they'd never given their kids such advice. Playing nice in the sandbox, for example. Even if the sandbox is an office filled with computers and coworkers instead of a play area filled with toys and sand, it's still important for Mom and Dad to "play nice" (whether or not the kids are actually watching).

One mother I know will shop at one store, only to return the items to another store where the price is higher. She makes a profit, but at what expense? Her kids are watching, after all, and are witnesses to her dishonest "accomplishment." How will she explain to them the importance of honesty and integrity, having demonstrated just the opposite? Her behavior is helping create a blueprint from which her kids will build their own lives.

Being a Ham Sandwich

Mom had just returned from my parent teacher conferences. I can't tell you what she reported back to me on my performance, but I can remember what she told me about her walk down the school halls.

She had run into Ray, the custodian, between teacher appointments. Having served as my homeroom mother over the years, Mom knew the school regulars pretty well. Naturally, Ray and my mom stopped to chat. When she came home, Mom informed me that she had just gotten a

BIG HAM SANDWICH

(In my family, a "ham sandwich" is our private code for something really **spectacular, super, wonderful.**)

Rather than reporting any teachers' insights, she relayed her conversation with Ray. He'd told her that I always greeted him with a smile and treated him nicely as he cleaned (apparently this was not always the case with other kids).

I was glad she thought I'd behaved in a Ham Sandwich sort of way, but I didn't understand why she was making such a **big deal**. I didn't realize that such "hello-ing" was not the norm. After all, my never-met-a-stranger mother responded to everybody with a smile and a friendly greeting! I was just imitating, as all kids do.

I suppose she didn't think about it, but witnessing her "in action" left a big—if subliminal—impression on me. I feel lucky to have had a love-overflowing figure to emulate. Even now, though I may not always remember to behave in such big-hearted ways, at least I know what I'm aiming for.

A Chance to Reflect

I came home from school one day, complaining about something completely unfair that a friend had done to (innocent little) me. My mother's response was shocking:

"If you don't like the way someone else is behaving, maybe you should see whether it's really something you don't like about yourself."

Huh?! Me?! Do something irritating or unfair? Oh, no, I was quite sure my mom had misunderstood me. After all, I was **RIGHT**! The other girl was **WRONG**!

That's when I got The Mirror Lesson. Mom explained to me how people can serve as mirrors for us, reflecting our strengths and weaknesses and offering us the chance to...

Look within and GROW

I see this remains yet another challenging lesson for me, because there are many times I really don't want to think that I would do THAT. Sometimes I wonder how far I've come since the eighth grade Mirror Lesson.

A few months ago, for instance, my husband and I were having a disagreement. He suggested that "Maybe our egos are getting in the way of clear communication."

I thought, **"WELL, MAYBE YOUR EGO, BUT CERTAINLY NOT MINE!"** wisely keeping that less-than-loving idea to myself.

When I cooled down, I realized—but not without smiling, at least—that what was really driving me nuts about him that day was something I'd been trying to change in myself for quite some time (obviously without raging success).

It turns out that Life does that...puts people in our lives to help identify those darned opportunities to "look within and grow." Sometimes, just to be sure we take full advantage of the lesson, we are actually related to those "opportunities."

We may not always like what we see in Life's mirrors, but the sooner we accept their gifts, the more we'll enjoy their company!

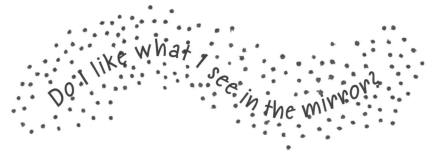

Do I like what I see in the mirror?

Inner Voice, Rejoice!

I didn't consider it so remarkable then, but thinking back I am surprised at how unusual it was for my mom to "let" me become a vegetarian. At age twelve, I requested sauerbraten for dinner one Saturday, because starting Sunday I would no longer be eating anything that ever had a mother.

This was in the '70s, when most people still viewed the four food groups as very cow-intensive. I'm certain my proclamation came as a surprise. (I am, after all, the granddaughter of a boot-and-hat-wearing cowboy—a meat-and-potatoes heritage not generally conducive to vegetarian progeny.) While Mom asked me questions about protein, she never doubted or made fun of my sincerity and intent.

I found out later that many of her friends had been shocked by her "permissiveness."

"How can you let her **do** that?"

they would, apparently, inquire. And she just answered,

"How can I **not**?"

39

She further informed her well-meaning "advisoracious" buddies that it was "Kelly's body, and she could decide for herself."

How could she let me make such a big life decision (I'm still meatless) so many years ago? I guess the real answer to "How can you let her DO that?" is that Mom always advised me to

Listen to Your Inner Voice.

She believed my Inner Voice would never lead me in the wrong direction. I guess she must have really believed that since **SHE** was willing to listen to my Inner Voice, too.

I haven't taken an actual poll, but I suspect that most mothers would have had a more meat-intensive **"ANSWER"** for their kids. Maybe that's because they've long since forgotten how to listen to their own Inner Voice, so they don't understand or remember the value in listening to a young person's intuition.

I think a lot of folks have let go of that "gut feeling" since it is so often

counterintuitive to Society's Way of Thinking. But there was my mom, going a step beyond listening to her own internally wired sound system and teaching me to listen to mine.

There is only one thing Mom made me promise about being vegetarian: I must never hop on any soap boxes for the "sake of" those folks who remain carnivorous. (My darling omnivore husband appreciates this policy.) **"Never waste your energy being against something,"** she explained. "Always be positive when you try to make a point." (It's a honey versus vinegar thing.)

uhhh... how 'bout some french fries instead?

I do hope this wisdom springs to mind the day my kids ask me for a Big Mac!

Ticket for Understanding

I don't remember all the details about this next story, but I still have **The Lesson** I took away. And I guess that's what this book is about anyway. The **details** aren't all that important. In fact, if they were, these lessons wouldn't be worth repeating. The thing is, though, the stuff I learned from my mom in specific situations turns out to be quite valuable in the **BIG PICTURE**.

little picture

BIG PICTURE

So here's what I remember. I was mad at my sister for losing the tickets to a family event. She had them on her lap and stood up. Poof, they disappeared.

When she tearfully reported the by-default cancellation of the family outing, I yelled at her for being so irresponsible. I'm sad to admit it, but yes, while my obviously upset sibling was "confessing" her sins to the family, I jumped right in and added to her feelings of remorse. After I finished, my mother gently pulled me to the side and asked me if I hadn't noticed that my sister was already upset. Sure, the tears were a pretty big clue.

"Then why," she inquired, "would you make her feel worse about a situation that wouldn't improve by your additional belittling? You should never hurt anyone else's heart."

Mom didn't yell, and she didn't condescend. I think she really, truly wondered how I could add to my sister's hurt heart. Of course, there was no great answer. There is **never** a good reason to kick someone when she's down.

Non Prom

In high school, Major World Issues more often seem to revolve around calls from the opposite sex and not getting a pimple on picture day than, say, oh, global peace or ending world hunger. I was not above pimple paranoia myself, so you can imagine that not getting an invite to **The Prom** was more than slightly devastating for me. I was absolutely positive that I would never have a date; **NOBODY** would want to be seen with me after such a large-scale humiliation.

ahh, world peace!

Even these many eons later, I remember my non-prom night distinctly (though the humiliation part has long since faded, I am happy to report). All my friends were there. In fact, "everybody" in the world was at the prom but poor little me. My mother tried to console me, but probably tired of my self-pity after a few hours. (She was certain I would actually survive the ordeal, a belief I did not share at the time.)

Fortunately for my ego and me, Mom had just bought the book **ILLUSIONS** and suggested that I read it. With no other pressing activities on my evening agenda (homework would have been too devastating an alternative at that point), I sat down to read. A couple of hours later, I had finished what would turn out to be one of my favorite books. That little gem shook me out of my misery like a ride on a roller coaster. The line that especially touched me was this one:

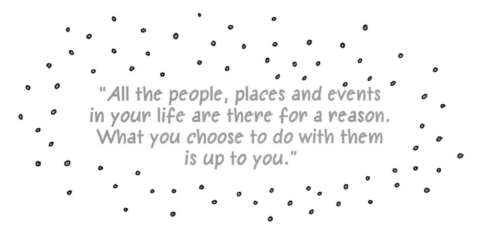

"All the people, places and events in your life are there for a reason. What you choose to do with them is up to you."

Another **bonk** on the head! That loneliest night, something really hit me about **CHOICE**. We all have it, as I've mentioned before, but we don't all use it.

I still call on that quote to help me remember that I don't have to be a victim. That I can create whatever magnificent morsel I want out of the ingredients the Universe puts in my pantry. It's up to me.

Me? Worry?

It was my first international flight. I had just graduated from high school and was on my way to study Spanish in Mexico. Back then, I was no expert on on-time departures. That's why the first plane for Guadalajara left without me.

Having realized my tardiness at the Departures board, I ran frantically to the ticket desk. The agent behind the counter rescheduled me, and directed me to relax and get ice cream with my family. So I did.

Let me say right here that my family members are hilarious. Pee-in-your-pants funny. So funny, in fact, that you might just forget your plane is taking off. And so I did.

Hee Hee! How hilarious! Ha Ha Ha oops...

Back at the ticket counter, my incredulous new friend reassigned me. Again. This time, however, my bags were already on their way.

"What do I do about my luggage?" I asked, worried that I'd have nothing cute to wear for summer school.

"Your luggage will be waiting for you in a special claims area at the Guadalajara airport," he assured me.

I wasn't buying his confidence; after all, it was supposed to have been oh-so-simple to get my buns on that plane.

"So you're SURE my bags will go to Guadalajara? I don't have to worry about them?" I really needed some wardrobe reassurance at that point.

In response, this never-saw-him-before-or-since airline employee handed me one of my **life's most influential lessons** so far...

"Well, I suppose you **COULD** worry about them if you wanted. You could torment yourself the entire flight to Mexico, once you finally get on the plane, that is. But all that worrying won't make them arrive any more safely."

Of course he was right. I could have worried from the second I (finally) got on that plane, but it would have had no effect on getting my bags to their south of the border destination.

How many times do we worry about things we have no influence over? I know I've festered over things like whether...

It would rain the day of our outdoor wedding

The flowers I'd sent to a friend in Phoenix would wilt on her doorstep before she got home

I'll be late, even though I'm already en route and doing everything possible to reach my destination on time

When I start such frivolous worrying, I remind myself of my first flight to Mexico, how I landed safely (a little late, but safe), and how all the hair-pulling or nail-biting in the world wouldn't have changed a thing.

So, while I **CAN** always worry, I now know I can **CHOOSE** not to.

Love to Go

Letters are great hard-copy reminders of the love we carry with us. Mom wrote me zillions of letters over the years, but one remains a favorite. She tucked it in a ribbon-sealed love bag, and I found it as I unpacked my *college suitcase*.

love bag

I have been known to pop that letter in luggage myself, so it might accompany me on other adventures...always reminding me of how very much I am loved.

I wonder how many parents have shared oh-so-similar thoughts about their own children, but never stopped to write them down? Given how much my mom's letters still mean to me, I will put **Write to My Kids** on my list of **Important Stuff to Remember**.

Letters expressing love can go both ways, of course. I'll never forget one "love letter" a friend of mine sent to his mother on his birthday. Yes, **HIS** birthday. Along with flowers. He wanted his mom to know how thankful he was for all she did to enable him to celebrate that day.

Why not send love notes on all sorts of occasions? A father could send a son a note on Father's Day, to thank his son for the chance to be his dad. Or what about a love note to say **"SORRY"** after an argument? Or maybe write one that says **"Just Because."**

There are lots of opportunities to express your love in writing. And the "residual value" is great; those words can be revisited year after year. To demonstrate just that, I've included my favorite Mom love letter on the following page. I thought it might be helpful for those of us less practiced in the ways of actually putting our feelings on paper. (By the way, she hopes you'll feel free to use whatever parts of the letter happen to ring your bell, as she got the idea from someone else before her!)

Oh Dear Kelly,

What shall we pack into all these boxes and suitcases?

There is so much stuff and you can't take it all with you...Some of this you won't need any more, but part of it I hope you will take with you wherever you go.

The faded corsages...they can be tossed, but not the memories they bring.

You can throw away most of the old notes and school papers, you will soon have notebooks full of new learning and new experiences. But save a few of the old notes and memories. They have given you a strong foundation for your new world.

In this pile are some tears from the growing pains that popped up from time to time. You don't need to pack those. There must always be new tears for new disappointments that are a natural part of life.

Always remember, you'll never be too old to cry...Like the song says, "Crying helps get the hurt out of you." As your mother, I hope there won't be many hurts, but I know that you have much strength within.

Nothing is going to come along that could knock you off your strong foundation. Your strong belief in God and yourself...Take that with you always.

And there's laughter! Those are the biggest piles of all. Thank you for those piles the most! Thank goodness there's enough for you to take a lot with you, and still leave loads for us.

I'm crying now, not because I don't want you to go. I'm crying because part of my life is ending, as I have always known it would. It's time...

Time for independence...

Time for responsibility...

Time for you to do your thing in your way...

Thank you my beautiful butterfly for all the joy you have brought to our family.

Into this "Love Bag" I have packed enough hugs and kisses to last a long time...and half my heart.

M

Guilt Is a Useless Emotion

My baby sister was visiting me at college when she witnessed me in the middle of a guilt-frenzy. I no longer recall the source of the guilt, I only remember lamenting at how guilty I'd feel if I did whatever that not-so-great something was.

Right there, in the living room of my four-roommate apartment, Katy put her hands on her ninth-grade hips and informed me:

Guilt is a
useless emotion.

Much like the **lightning bolt** that hit me when I was trying to get my buns and bags to Guadalajara, Katy's epiphany zapped me right between the eyes.

She had a really good point, you know. As a motivator, guilt ain't so great. I mean, who wants help or love or **anything** from someone who is just responding to guilt? It's SO much better to be motivated by **LOVE**, or the **desire to see someone succeed**, or happiness—any sort of positive stimulator.

Katy's insight has come in handy throughout the years. For instance, while fund-raising for nonprofit organizations, I could see that people responded much more $$favorably$$ to positive requests than to requests that tried to guilt them into forking over donations. So I kept my requesting messages tied to the great benefits of generosity, rather than the negative repercussions of **not** giving.

Dear Donor,
Thanks to your generosity, 3,299 acres of rainforest were saved last week. Great going, and thanks!
It feels good to be successful in our efforts to help the...

Parking Lot Karma

You wouldn't normally count on a Love Lesson from UPS, but like I said earlier, opportunities to learn can show up where they are least expected (including, for example, parking lots).

Back in the days when my Precious Possessions could be shipped in a few boxes, UPS sent them back and forth to college. One pre-fall semester day, I schlepped my boxes to a nearby UPS office and waited my turn. At the weigh-in counter, after revealing the contents, I was informed that UPS "isn't in the moving business." The employee was nice and apologetic, but there was nothing she could do (especially now that she knew the contents—another case for ignorance being bliss).

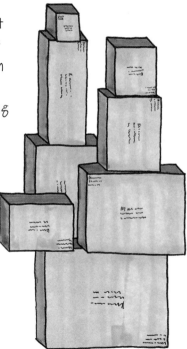

After confirming that no exceptions could be made—the manager was temporarily out of the office—I thanked the lady behind the counter and began to cart my stuff back to my car. As I was reloading my car, a man approached and started to help me with the boxes. But he was loading in the wrong direction; instead of helping me put the boxes back in my car, he was putting my boxes back on the cart. So I explained the situation.

"Did you yell at the woman?"

he asked intently.

"Did you cause a scene?"

I told him she was so nice and trying so hard, that there was really no need for causing an uproar. (Though I confess I have not always been above scene-making.)

"Really, no scene?"

He didn't seem to believe me.

Upon reaffirming that I had left the UPS office without so much as an "I'll report you" threat, he revealed that he was the office manager. Since I'd been so nice, he would override the rules and allow me to ship my stir-fry wok and my wardrobe back to school.

Had my mother's advice to "be nice to everyone" not been humming through my brain cells like a subliminal mantra, I would have had to send my treasures in a much less convenient way. But she was right whenever she would tell me:

You sure catch more flies with honey than with vinegar.

I'm not saying that niceness is without its own intrinsic rewards. After all, being nice...and calm...and friendly feels a lot better on my insides than revving my heart's RPMs.

Don't we all feel that way?

Thinking Makes It So

Mom used to tell me,

Things aren't good
or bad, they just "are."
It's what you make of
them that counts.

She wasn't the only one with this train of thought. A few years earlier,
Shakespeare wrote,

There is nothing either
good or bad but
thinking makes it so.
—Hamlet

Quite a few other wise people have made the same point over the years...

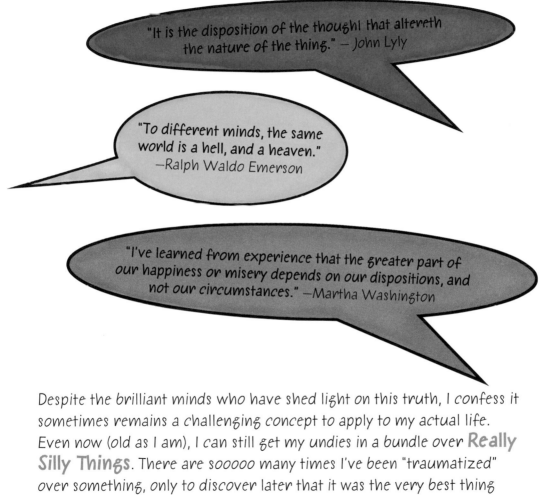

"It is the disposition of the thought that altereth the nature of the thing." — John Lyly

"To different minds, the same world is a hell, and a heaven." —Ralph Waldo Emerson

"I've learned from experience that the greater part of our happiness or misery depends on our dispositions, and not our circumstances." —Martha Washington

Despite the brilliant minds who have shed light on this truth, I confess it sometimes remains a challenging concept to apply to my actual life. Even now (old as I am), I can still get my undies in a bundle over **Really Silly Things**. There are sooooo many times I've been "traumatized" over something, only to discover later that it was the very best thing that could have happened to me. (I'm sure you can come up with a few

59

examples yourself. See what I mean? This lesson's a toughy!)

A memorable lesson in this whole **attitude-as-situation-definer** thing happened when I was studying in Taiwan. While Taiwan has a lot to offer in terms of culture and language-building opportunities, for a recent college graduate, it provided very little in the way of dates, or similar friends, or anything like a "real life." * I wasn't having a great time there. **OK**, I was miserable.

Then my friend Helen came to visit. Helen is originally from Taiwan, and now lives in the U.S. with her darling husband and kids. While I was there practicing my 中文 she visited her parents.

Thankfully, she visited me too, because—in addition to guiding me to the best food spots—she taught me to "see the good side" of Taiwan. While she was on that tiny, people-dense island, I witnessed the place in a completely different light. Through her eyes, everything was

* I should say that this was light-years ago, when blondes in Taipei were a "stare-at-and-follow" oddity. Relatively few "foreigners" were studying there at the time.

We had a fabulous time together. Then she returned to the States. I was sad to see her go, but she left with me such a treasure; Taiwan—and my way of seeing things—would **NEVER** be the same! Helen reminded me that

you can **CHOOSE** to be happy

This wasn't something I hadn't heard before, but I sure hadn't been applying it to my life in Taiwan!

Taiwan before Helen

Taiwan after Helen

After Helen flew off, I realized that **TAIWAN** hadn't changed one iota. I had done the changing. Or should I say my **outlook** had changed? Same country. Same Kelly (more or less). **Different perspective**.

Thinking made it so.

Childlike

Mom always giggled a lot. She still does. She can stand on her head like a pro.

She loves cotton candy and parades. When I ask her how her day went, she'll tell me it was "dreamy." And when she talks to little kids, she always makes sure to squat so she's at their level.

I think these habits are why her father used to ask her (when she was in her forties):

AREN'T YOU EVER GOING TO GROW UP?

For my benefit, and the benefit of those around her, I hope her answer is always, **"NO!"**

Don't be confused, though. I'm not talking about **CHILDISH**. There's a big difference between "like" and "ish" when those suffixes attach themselves to "child." Child**LIKE** is someone who still knows how to giggle. Someone who remembers joy and unlimited possibilities, and **YES**!!!!! And keeps them fresh and sparkling in her life. (Cotton candy apparently helps in this process.)

Child-ISH ≠ Child-LIKE

Child**ISH**, on the other hand, has more to do with tantrums and selfishness, not taking responsibility, and forgetting that joy is our natural state. You can be on the planet a lot of years and still be childish (as an old boss of mine proved on a regular basis).

Besides generally having a lot more fun, another good thing about being childlike is that you don't have to know all the answers. You don't have to **BE RIGHT**. Instead, you can stay open to all the **Possible Answers** if you don't already think you know them. This creates a lot of potential for **Great Stuff** to happen.

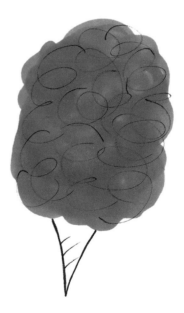

Oscar Wilde said, "I am not young enough to know everything." Hmmm, and he never even met my mom!

Self-Induced Stress

Through some apparent genetic mutation, I arrived on the planet feeling like there was a lot to do and never enough time to do it. My mother, however, remains unfettered by schedules or timing. This fact is **(a)** a source of great stress to me still, preferring timeliness as I do; and **(b)** probably one of the Reasons she's been such a wonderful teacher to me all these years.

Whether it was grades in school or piano recital nerves, my mom has never nurtured my tendency to get stressed out. She has always lovingly reminded me that

All
stress
is
self-induced

In the midst of having a **stress-out**, I've found that this has not necessarily been her most endearing saying. Likely that's because it's so painfully true.

In our more clear moments, we can all probably look back and see that many upsetting situations were, in the end, completely unstressworthy (particularly if one professes, as I do, to believe that **All Things Happen for a Reason**).

Sometimes I wonder whether God sits back and chuckles at our insistence upon stress and worry.

My sister Katy tells of arriving at a beauty salon one day, just as a little boy went in to get his first haircut. Judging from his screams, he was not thrilled by the experience. Every time the scissors came close to his head, he broke out in eardrum-smashing shrieks. He was petrified of those scissors and what they might do.

Everyone in the beauty shop was amused by his fear of something as "obviously" harmless as scissors in the hands of a competent professional.

As Katy sat watching the seemingly no-reason-for-it terror, she wondered whether that's what the angels think when we hyper humans stress out...

"Why's that guy screaming? It's just the karmic equivalent of a haircut!"

Expanding Your Focus

In case you haven't guessed by now, my mom has always been a very positive person. Definitely the glass half-full type. Even though she has her own "bag of rocks" (like we all do), she tends to **focus** on the good parts. I think this is why so many people love to be around her. And it's my theory (not yet scientifically confirmed) that her lifelong positive focus is why she has so few wrinkles!

Have you ever known anyone who spends **lots of time** telling you why things are going wrong in her life, talking about all the people who are causing her to be miserable, to not succeed, to fill-in-the-blank? I call these people "Negative Norma" or "Negative Norm" (depending on the appropriate gender, of course). And I notice I don't rush to return their phone calls when they leave a message on my answering machine. After all, I already know what I'm going to hear!

Hello...this is Negative Norma...
Are you there, Kelly?

I once heard Arnold Patent (a wise writer and lecturer) say,

WHAT YOU FOCUS ON EXPANDS.

Isn't that the truth?! Those people who go on and on about their woes always seem to have plenty more material to complain about! It's like they expand their own misery. **Very exhausting stuff**.

On the other hand, there are people like my friend Sue. I've known her for ages, and I've yet to hear her spout a Negative Norma phrase. I don't think it's a coincidence that things in her life seem to go smoothly! I'm not saying she hasn't hit a few speedbumps, but they always **stay** speedbumps; they never turn into Mount Kilimanjaro! (no molehills into mountains!) She doesn't spend time making mountains of misery; she's too busy focusing on the potential good stuff in front of her.

MOLEHILL   MOUNTAINS

Funny. I notice I always call Sue back right away; I can't wait to tune into what interesting things she has to say!

Thank You Very Much

Along the lines of focusing on the positive, one **Very Practical Habit** Mom taught me was writing thank-you notes. I know some people dread doing that, but, actually, those mannerly messages are a great way to focus on abundance. The abundance of friendship, of happy times, of wonderful surprises.

In writing thank-you notes, you get another chance to concentrate on the kindness someone has generously shared with you. It's important to send those **grateful vibes** into the Universe, too, because whatever you're busy putting out there, you can be sure it will all *come back to you*...

MAGNIFIED

There are a few practical pointers I'd like to offer when writing a meaningful thank-you note. First, be timely. While one of my friends tries to respond before it's time to dust the gift, another sends off a thank-you the minute her gift-giver leaves. While dust accumulation is a fairly uninspired cue for good manners, I definitely think you can go to bed before you take pen in hand. (If too many nights pass—like a season's worth—it's probably best to forego sending a reminder of your etiquette lapse.)

Second, try not to begin a note of appreciation with that completely boring word combo:

"Thank you very much for the___..."

Surely our brain cells can respond more creatively to someone having spent time, energy, and/or cash on our behalf. Consider a different kind of starter, such as

"How sweet of you to remember I collect lavender teacups..."

or

"How did you know I've always wanted to go on a cruise down the Nile?"

I guess the point here is that someone went beyond the norm to do something special for you. It's just plain nice to reciprocate.

The F Word:
FORGIVENESS

Mom did her best to teach me about forgiving others. One creative technique she showed me was to place my "challenge" in a pink cloud. The "challenge" could be a person or a situation, anything negative that was taking up space in my heart. Then I could just let that now-less-offensive pink-clouded challenge float happily away to its proper place in the Universe. In the "grown-up" language I sometimes use these days, I'd say the lesson she taught me was about not throwing my energy away.

place forgiveness thought here

I think the Forgiveness thing is still one of my most challenging lessons, though I'm not quite sure why. (Apologies, Mom.) Maybe it's because I sometimes care more about being **RIGHT** than being HAPPY. And oftentimes, I've noticed, I practice "being right" on the people I'm closest to—my relatives.

Once, in a lecture by the wise and wonderful Marianne Williamson, I heard her talk about how our family members can help us rub off our "rough edges." She had a great point. After all, you can't dump a brother or an aunt the way you can punt a boyfriend who no longer fits your definition of "dream boat."

But unless you move to the Ukraine or enroll in the FBI's Witness Protection Program, chances are high that you'll be bumping up next to your relatives for years...and years...and years. And, chances are, throughout all those years of bumping, some feelings are bound to get bruised. That's where the **F** word comes in: *forgiveness*.

Sometimes I think I must still be a **forgiveness kindergartner**. How do I know I'm no master of true forgiveness? Because when I think of certain offending persons or incidents I still let some of my energy leak away...even with the help of pink clouds!

Here's an example. Try it yourself. Think of something completely neutral,

like a bicycle wheel

or a towel

or Switzerland.

Now think of the last time your brother screamed obscenities into the receiver and then hung up on you. Or your aunt asked you how you could possibly gain so much weight in such a short time. See what I mean? Did you feel your energy sneaking away from you?

In her book **ANATOMY OF THE SPIRIT**, Caroline Myss says,

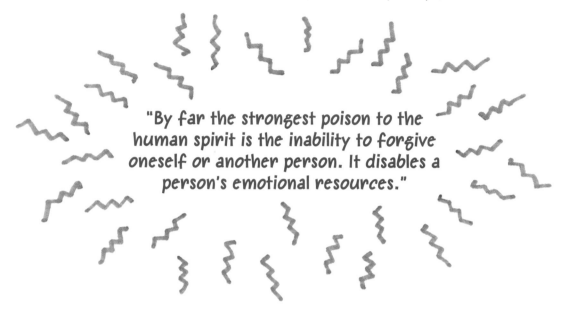

"By far the strongest poison to the human spirit is the inability to forgive oneself or another person. It disables a person's emotional resources."

When you leak energy by being mad at someone, it produces nothing positive for anybody, and you are the one who suffers the most. You definitely weaken your emotional resources.

Maybe the next time you need some **resource reinforcement**, try calling in a pink cloud and see how it works for you. It may take some practice (as I can surely attest), but it beats wasting your precious energy on negativity!

Swoosh*

Most of the lessons I've shared here have been

BEWARE: **LIGHTHEARTED** does not necessarily mean **LIGHTWEIGHT**. These little chapters in my life and in this book have affected the very core of who I am and how I respond to **What Life Brings**, even in the toughest of times.

As I mentioned earlier, I started writing this book to remember and emulate some really wonderful parenting examples. When I was pregnant with our first baby, I hoped to raise her with the same **BIG LOVE** I had been so lucky to know. Unfortunately, I didn't have that chance. Before she arrived, we lost our daughter to a broken heart. I truly believed my own heart would break.

* "Swoosh" was what we called our daughter when she was in utero, since that's what her speedy little heart sounded like at the time: swoosh, swoosh, swoosh, swoosh...

In the middle of the heartache, I REALLY wanted to find An Answer. I wanted her life to have been for a **"REASON."** I wanted to make some sense out of all that confusion. Ultimately, that is why I wanted to create and share this book of my mom's Love Lessons. It is our not-to-be baby's gift to me, and hopefully to you.

Throughout the nightmare, my mother, brimming with faith and love, helped me seek out blessing in the pain and create something positive from what seemed immeasurably negative. In her expert letter-writing way, she sent my husband and me the letter on the following page.

My mom didn't say, "Don't feel bad," or declare that "Everything will be all right." No, she acknowledged the pain and tried to help us find our way through it. By encouraging us to look for the gifts, she helped us focus in a healing direction:

Toward the Positive.

Toward the Light.

Thank you, again, Mom. And thank you, Swoosh.

Dear Kelly, Dear Bob,

Your little angel who didn't quite make it brought some wonderful gifts we will have forever. As for me, I got to experience a new kind of love I never would have known without her. And the love lessons she brought to me via her beautiful mother will always be among my greatest treasures...for that I will be forever grateful.

I know she brought many blessings to you two. As time passes, I'm sure we'll become aware of other gifts she brought—gifts we'll always have, no matter what!

We are so grateful that you have each other...your amazing love for each other...your inner strengths, which are many...your friends and family members to nurture you, to support you, and to be there for you as you heal together. We shall have many more joys to share, I know. But your sorrow—especially your sorrow—we share that with you now. And, oh, our hearts hurt for you. Your sorrow is ours.

Please know how much you are loved.

Please be comforted by how much you are loved.

XOXO

M

Responsible Faith

Trust in Allah and tie up your camel.
—An old Sufi saying

God helps those who help themselves.*
—Anonymous

Ride the Cosmic Wave, but never sign a contract without reading all the fine print.
—Mom

I wouldn't do these lessons justice if I didn't bring up the Responsibility part. Sure, Mom has reminded me countless times to Trust the Universe and Consider the Lilies. I noticed, however, in the midst of her own trusting, that she didn't just hang out on the couch eating bonbons, waiting for **Really Good Things** to happen to her. She is, shall we say, esoteric but practical.

*Everybody thinks this comes from the Bible, but nobody really knows the originator of this famous phrase!

I know lots of people who are esoteric. I know even more people who are practical. There are very few, however, who have found the balance. Even with her fabulous example in my life, I can't say I've got the balance down like Mom does. But it's fun to practice, especially when I stay conscious of all these precious Love Lessons I've been taught.

After Words

So here they are, some Love Lessons recorded for you. They are not all directly from my mom, but she inspired them. As all the quotes I've included prove, however, she's (fortunately) not the only one with **Really Good Insights**. Great ideas on How to Be are all over the place! From Shakespeare to Sugar Ray Robinson (who said, **"I've always believed that you can think positive just as well as you can think negative"**), there are lots of folks willing to shine a little light on our souls.

I hope you and your heart have gained something from reading these lessons. I know I sure got a lot out of remembering them and writing them down! I don't know what zapped you, but for me, the two main Love Lessons that really stuck centered around **CHOICE** and **FOCUS**. Even if you never met my mom, you can certainly decide to **CHOOSE** happiness and **FOCUS** on the good stuff. Because, as I firmly believe,

What you choose to focus on will always expand.

Acknowledgments

Mom always said,

When it's right, it's easy.

If that's the case, this project was 100% right!

Creating this book was fun and exciting. This, of course, was due in part to how good it made me feel writing about all of the beautiful lessons from my past (thanks, Mom). But the help and support of some outrageously wonderful people along the way also contributed to the whole positive experience...

My husband: Despite the fact that most events in his own professional world of engineering move logically from points **A** to **B** to **C** and so on, he was always supportive and enthusiastic about my writing a book and actually getting it published.

Jo Ann Deck: The kind and creative visionary at Celestial Arts who gave Love Lessons the green light.

Annie Nelson: Project editor extraordinaire. Her patience, sense of humor, and attention to detail made the "work" of polishing up a complete joy.

Kelly Corbet lives in Northern California with her darling husband and their new son. She practices the Love Lessons she already knows on them and, fortunately, they teach her even more.

Before the Universe sent her down the book-writing path, she earned her Master's degree from Harvard. She studied international environmental policy while there and afterward, used that knowledge to help start-up and multinational companies make cleaner products for the global market.

These days when she's not gardening or contacting her representatives about organic food regulations or nuclear waste, she writes up a storm. **Love Lessons from My Mom** is her first book, but more are on the way!

For more information, visit http://www.kellycorbet.com